THE MUSIC OF VICTOR HERBERT

Includes all the songs recorded by
Beverly Sills and Andre Kostelanetz on
Angel Album SFO-37160

AH! SWEET MYSTERY OF LIFE
(The Dream Melody)

Lyric by
RIDA JOHNSON YOUNG

Music by
VICTOR HERBERT

love a-lone that rules for aye! For 'tis love, and love a-lone, the world is

seek-ing, For 'tis love, and love a-lone that can re-pay! 'Tis the

an-swer, 'tis the end and all of liv-ing!_ For it is love a-lone that rules for

aye!_____

ITALIAN STREET SONG

Lyric by
RIDA JOHNSON YOUNG

Music by
VICTOR HERBERT

Ah! my heart is back in Na-po-li, __ Dear Na-po-li, __ dear Na-po-li, __ and I seem to hear a-gain in dreams __ her re-vel-ry, __ her sweet re-vel-ry __ The man-do-li-nas play-ing

NOTE-OBBLIGATO TO BE SUNG WITH 2nd CHORUS ONLY
Allegro moderato

Boom, boom, aye, La, la, la, Ha, ha, ha, Zing, boom aye.

La, la, la, la, ha, ha, ha, zing, zing, aye. ___ aye. ___ aye. ___

Segue to A

Fine

A to B may omited

La, la, la, la ___

La, la, la, la, ___

A KISS IN THE DARK

Lyric by
B.G. DeSYLVA

Music by
VICTOR HERBERT

Refrain *a little slower*

Kiss in the dark Was to him just a lark, But to me 'twas a thrill su - preme! Just a

EVERY DAY IS LADIES' DAY WITH ME

Lyric by
HENRY BLOSSOM

Music by
VICTOR HERBERT

I should like, with-out un-due re-it-er-a-tion of the e-go, To ex-
It's a frightfull thing to think of all the hearts that I have broken, Al-tho'

plain, how ve-ry hard I find it is to make my pay go 'Round a-
each one fell in love with me with-out the slight-est to-ken, That my

mong my vul-gar cre-dit-ors I'm fear-ful-ly in debt, For I al-ways have af-ford-ed an-y-
fa-tal gift of beau-ty had in-flamed her lit-tle heart, But I found that some small fa-vor al-ways

thing that I could get! But I must say I've en-joyed the best of
seemed to ease the smart. A po-si-tion for a cous-in or a

what there is in life; I've been luck-y in my love af-fairs I've
loan to dear pa-pa; Just a dain-ty dia-mond neck-lace or a

ne-ver had a wife! I can sum-mon lit-tle int'-rest in the
pret-ty mo-tor car. But I don't be-grudge the col-lar-ets and

dry af-fairs of state, And the bus'-ness-men who call on me are
neck-la-ces or pearls, All the mon-ey that I ev-er saved is

rall. *a tempo* REFRAIN.

cold-ly left to wait! For ev-e-ry day is la-dies' day with
what Iv'e spent on girls! For ev-e-ry day is la-dies' day with

16

KISS ME AGAIN

Lyric by
HENRY BLOSSOM

Music by
VICTOR HERBERT

see you a - gain, as you gazed in my eyes With joy_____ all a - light!_____ So

fond-ly you'd fold me as soft - ly you told me Of Love through the star-sprink-led night._____

Valse lente

Sweet sum-mer breeze, whis-per-ing trees, Stars shin-ing soft - ly a - bove;_____

Ros - es in bloom, waft-ed per-fume, Sleep-y birds dream-ing of

THINE ALONE

Lyric by
HENRY BLOSSOM

Music by
VICTOR HERBERT

Moderato espressivo

Tell me! Why is there a doubt with-in thy heart, my own! Tell me,

why? I but fear the time will come when we must part! A -

loss the world could not a - tone! Be -

lov'd I swear that I will e'er be true And for - ev - er, thine __ a -

lone! _____

lone! _____ (Optional ending) Thine a - lone! _____

I'M FALLING IN LOVE WITH SOMEONE

Lyric by
RIDA JOHNSON YOUNG

Music by
VICTOR HERBERT

cause, My spir - its are tru - ly un - ru - ly._____ For I'm
queer, But I heart - i - ly hope I don't show it._____

REFRAIN.
poco a poco.

fall - ing in love with some one, some

one girl;_____ I'm fall - ing in love with some

INDIAN SUMMER

Lyric by
AL DUBIN

Music by
VICTOR HERBERT

WHEN YOU'RE AWAY

Lyric by
HENRY BLOSSOM

Music by
VICTOR HERBERT

me there still can be but you! Come weal or woe, my love is true! Ah!

dear one, if you on - ly knew My heart, when you're a - way.

Slower, starting very softly

When you're a - way, dear, how wear - y the lone - some hours! ___

Sun - shine seems gray, dear! The frag - rance has left the flow'rs! ___

'NEATH THE SOUTHERN MOON

Lyric by
RIDA JOHNSON YOUNG

Music by
VICTOR HERBERT

hearts, you rule, you rule for - ev - er, Queen of hearts, whose pow'r shall ev - er

grow.___ No, no, no, no! I'll look_ I'll see no fur - ther! ___ For if 'tis

lost, I can - not, dare not know.

Piu lento, molto appassionato

'Neath the South.-ern moon, Oh, love so warm and ten - der!

MOONBEAMS
(A Serenade)

Lyric by
HENRY BLOSSOM

Music by
VICTOR HERBERT

Moderato

pp dolcissimo

Andantino semplice

pp

L.H.
(Optional Accompaniment)

pp

The day is gone and the night comes on, And the birds have sought their nest,_____ The shad - ows fall in a

bring me the mes-sage he fain would__ send, I know he is dream-ing of me!_____

Moon-beams shin-ing__ soft a - bove Let me beg of__ you, Find the one I__

dear - ly love! Tell him I'll e'er be__ true! Fate may part us, years may pass,

Fut-ure all un - known! Still my love shall ev - er prove Faith-ful to him a - lone.__

THE STREETS OF NEW YORK
(In Old New York)

Lyric by
HENRY BLOSSOM

Music by
VICTOR HERBERT

45

I WANT WHAT I WANT WHEN I WANT IT

Lyric by
HENRY BLOSSOM

Music by
VICTOR HERBERT

48

49

TOYLAND

Lyric by
GLEN MacDONOUGH

Music by
VICTOR HERBERT

Very slow and dreamily

When
you've grown up, my dears ___ And are as old as I ___ You'll
you've grown up, my dears ___ There comes a drear-y day ___ When

oft-en pon-der on the years That roll so swift-ly by, my dears, that
'mid the locks of black ap-pears The first pale gleam of gray, my dears, the

52

GYPSY LOVE SONG
(Slumber On, My Little Gypsy Sweetheart)

Lyric by
HARRY B. SMITH

Music by
VICTOR HERBERT

54

BECAUSE YOU'RE YOU!

Lyric by
HENRY BLOSSOM

Music by
VICTOR HERBERT

58

EILEEN!
(Alanna Asthore)

Lyric by
HENRY BLOSSOM

Music by
VICTOR HERBERT

Moderato

I'm in love! I'm in love with a slip of a girl! And if I should be mer-ry or sad, I don't know! For my heart is a-fire, and my head is a-whirl! Yet I'm suf-frin' for her so I'm

ROMANY LIFE
(Czardas)

Lyric by
HARRY B. SMITH

Music by
VICTOR HERBERT

We have a home 'neath the for-est shades, Nev-er an-y oth-er_____ have we._____

Nev-er an-y oth-er_____ have we._____ Our camp-fires glow in the nooks and glades,

Where our tents are white_____ to see._____ Where our tents are white___ to see._____

MARCH OF THE TOYS

Lyric by
JOHN ALAN HAUGHTON

Music by
VICTOR HERBERT

Allegro molto moderato sempre pesante

69

70

I MIGHT BE YOUR ONCE-IN-A-WHILE

Lyric by
ROBERT B. SMITH

Music by
VICTOR HERBERT

stray. _____ But frank-ness is due to one Who
one. _____ I fear it's lo - cal - i - ty May

craves my ev-'ry kiss; _____ So I make it plain in
change from day to day. _____ It is ev-'ry where, now

rit. **Refrain**

my re-frain, That the best I can do is this: _____ I
here, now there, That is why I'm o-bliged to say: _____ I

rit. *p*

Poco meno
a tempo

might be your "once-in-a-while"__ I might see you

molto espress
a tempo

74

I CAN'T DO THE SUM

Lyric by
GLEN MAC DONOUGH

Music by
VICTOR HERBERT

mates were al-most six feet high, And the bos'-n near the same, Would
quite for-got the steer - ing gear, On her hon-eyed lips to sup, How
bill of fare were thir-teen nine-ty five, And poor Har-old had but four, How
naught but sun-ny out - side rooms, In a neigh-bor-hood of tone, How
if with ev-'ry pound of tea, He will give two cut glass plates, How

THE CHILDREN.

you sub-tract or mul - ti-ply, To find the cap-tains name? Oh!__
soon could twen-ty men with brooms, Sweep Clare and Gwen-nie up? Oh!__
ma - ny things would Har-old strike, Be-fore he struck the floor? Oh!__
old would those ten chil-dren be, Be-fore they found a home? Oh!__
soon would Wil-lie break his face, On his new roll-er skates? Oh!__

Oh_____ Oh!__
Oh_____ Oh!__
Oh_____ Oh!__
Oh_____ Oh!__
Oh_____ Oh!__

SWEETHEARTS

Lyric by
ROBERT B. SMITH

Music by
VICTOR HERBERT

ROSE OF THE WORLD

Lyric by
GLEN MAC DONOUGH

Music by
VICTOR HERBERT

85

THE ISLE OF OUR DREAMS

Lyric by
HENRY BLOSSOM

Music by
VICTOR HERBERT

DORIS.

When my heart grows faint and wea-ry, ____ when the

world goes sad-ly ill, ____ It is sweet to hear you,

dreams, dear, there is nev-er a sor-row or pain, ____ Eve-ry

trou-ble and care quick-ly van-ish-es there and

all is made hap-py ____ a-gain. ____ So we'll

JEANNETTE AND HER LITTLE WOODEN SHOES

Lyric by
ROBERT B. SMITH

Music by
VICTOR HERBERT

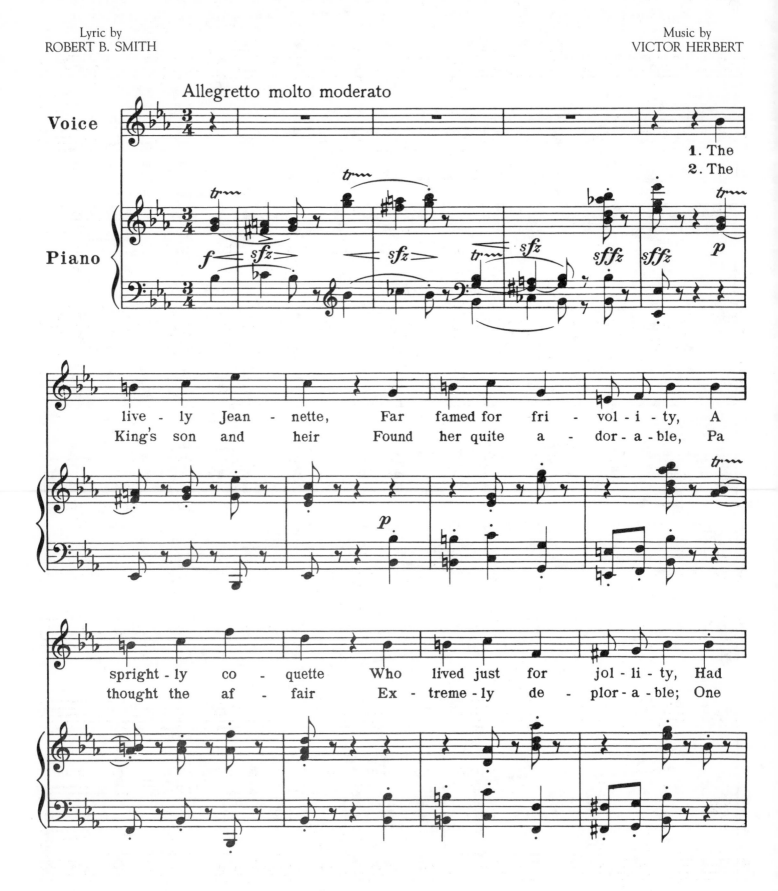

shoes._ Then the lads, half a - sleep, oh how jeal - ous they'd
fro;___ And he might be pur - su - ing those two lov - ers
p
poco rit.
a tempo
get, And they'd say to them - selves, "Who is out with Jean - nette?"
yet, But those wood - en shoe - tracks in the snow spell'd Jean - nette!
poco rit.
a tempo
sfz
Clip clop clop! Clip clop clop! O - ver the tiles. Her
Clip clop clop! Clip clop clop! There in the snow Her
feet were pe - tite, But you heard her for miles,_ With her
feet so pe - tite, Showed them which way to go,___ With her

pit-ter, pit-ter, pat-ter, clip clop clop, gos-sip pur-sues The
pit-ter, pit-ter, pat-ter, clip clop clop, they found the clues, And Jean-

se-crets be-trayed by Jean - nette's wood-en shoes!
nette lost her Prince through the prints of her shoes!

Wooden-shoe Dance

D.C.

ART IS CALLING FOR ME
(I Want To Be A Prima Donna)

Lyric by
HARRY B. SMITH

Music by
VICTOR HERBERT

98

TRAMP! TRAMP! TRAMP!

Lyric by
RIDA JOHNSON YOUNG

Music by
VICTOR HERBERT

Allegro marcato

We've hunt - ed the wolf in the for - est, We've
We've ranged o'er the North in the win - ter, We've

raid - ed the pi - rates at sea,____ We have no in - den - ture, we're
an - swered the call of the wild,____ We heard the wolf call - ing when

TO THE LAND OF MY OWN ROMANCE

Lyric by
HARRY B. SMITH

Music by
VICTOR HERBERT

Only in vi - sions of dream - land I met you, The one love, the true love di - vine.

You know and I know we all have had fan - cies, We think we're in love for a - while.

Vain - ly I tried, but I could not for - get you, I've
Look - ing in eyes that al - lure with their glanc - es, We

found you, at last you are mine!
yield to the charm of a smile.

cres - - - - cen - - - - do
I hear your voice and look in - to your eyes, To -
Fan - cies are ros - es that soon fade a - way, We
cres - - - cen - - - do

geth - er we'll find Par - a - dise.
all find the one love, some day.
rit.

REFRAIN *(molto espress)*

Land of ro - mance, so near, so far, There dreams will

all come true. _____ Thru the dark night fate's

sil - ver star Guid - ed to love and you. _____

And when your eyes looked in - to mine

NEAPOLITAN LOVE SONG
(T'amo!)

Lyric by
HENRY BLOSSOM

Music by
VICTOR HERBERT

PRETTY AS A PICTURE

Lyric by
ROBERT B. SMITH

Music by
VICTOR HERBERT

115